A Horse Named Sugar

Jillian Connolly

Illustrated By: Frances Espanol

Kimber~
Always follow
your dreams and
don't ever give up!
♡ Jill & Sugar♡

Copyright © 2015 by Jillian Connolly. 710881

LCCN:		2015907093
ISBN:	SoftCover	978-1-5035-6728-3
	HardCover	978-1-5035-6730-6
	EBook	978-1-5035-6729-0

Print information available on the last page

Rev. date: 05/04/2015

To order additional Copies of this book, Contact:
Xlibris
1-888-795-4274
www.Xlibris.Com
Orders@Xlibris.com

Dedication

I would like to dedicate this book to my very special niece, Angela.
In addition, I want to send out a giant thank you to my parents, Mike & Terry
Connolly for all of their help and support, and to God, as it is only with help
from above that any of these dreams or this great horse has come about.

Photo Credit
WT Bruce, thank you for allowing me to purchase and use the beautiful
action photo of Sugar & I from the Pendleton Roundup for publicity.

Late in the spring, many years ago, a pretty sorrel filly with a flaxen mane and tail was born. Cute as a button and very fancy, her curly blonde hair went everywhere! Of course, her name would be Sugar, for she was sweet as sugar.

Sugar grew and grew, but not very big very fast. She was a tiny little horse and many people would comment about the "little pony" and wondered what she would grow up to do. Sugar soon grew into her agile long legs. She ran and played in the pasture, making friends with the birds and the frogs. She even chased a rabbit or two.

All too soon, it was time to be ridden. Sugar wanted her freedom back! She wanted to play in the pasture with the others, she did not want to be saddled, ridden or trained. Sugar was ridden in the mountains, over the rocks, through the hills, and crossed streams. Then it was time to learn the clover leaf pattern. Sugar was asked to turn barrels, three of them. She quickly mastered this greatly pleasing herself and her rider.

Sugar began to love her job. Turning barrels and running was fun and easy. She continued to grow, becoming a beautiful and powerful barrel racing horse. Faster and faster, Sugar learned to run the barrel racing pattern. She won lots of money and prizes. Everyone stopped to give her treats and pet her. Sugar loved her rider and they became a very good team.

Then one cold spring day, she couldn't breathe. Coughing and coughing, Sugar fell to her knees. The vet looked Sugar over and said there was fluid in her lungs. Sugar stayed in a stall for a long time while she healed. In the fall, she was ready to train again and began to practice. Of course she blew the other horses away! Sugar ran and was even more determined than ever to be great!

The next spring, when rodeo season began, Sugar was ready. She loved the rodeos! The excitement, the energy, the noise! Nothing could be more fun than doing what she loved and having so many people to cheer for her during her seventeen seconds of fame! Sugar ran and ran. She traveled with her rider all over. Sometimes it was cold. Sometimes it was hot. Sugar ran in the rain, snow and wind. She loved to run and loved her job. Sugar was very good and made her rider very proud.

One hot day at a rodeo, Sugar slipped. She finished the race and in a good time too, but something was wrong. Ouch! Her leg was warm and puffy. Again she had to stay in a stall to heal. Sugar grew bitter and angry that she was not able to barrel race. She pawed and paced, and nibbled on the ground and posts.

She woke up with the tummy ache one cool fall morning and didn't feel well. Sugar's stomach was hurting badly. The vet said she would need surgery to get all the sand out of her belly. This scared Sugar, but when she woke up after the surgery the stomach ache was gone! She was thankful that the vet was able to make the hurting go away. She would be more careful now. No more eating sand on the ground!

It was not long at all, and Sugar and her rider were able to train and run again. Sugar tried even harder than she had before. She ran like the wind, as if she had angel's wings. Her steps were flawless and she was once again a great barrel racing horse.

MC Cattle Company
Grimes
Veterinary Services
Grimes
Veterinary Services

So many people came to watch her run, to admire her. Sugar was happy again, doing what she loved. She still runs today, like the wind, and is one of the fastest turning barrel racing horses there ever was. Keep an eye out, you might just see her at the next rodeo, and if you do, make sure you cheer extra loud!

Made in the USA
Lexington, KY
14 May 2015